The Zen Mama's Book of Quotes

A Collection Of Thoughts And Wisdom
Throughout The Ages

Smile, breathe and go slowly -

Betsy McLa Henry

ALSO BY BETSY MCKEE HENRY
How To Be A Zen Mama

The Zen Mama's Book of Quotes

A Collection Of Thoughts And Wisdom
Throughout The Ages

By Betsy McKee Henry

Zen Mama Publishing
Denver, Colorado

Cover Design by Betsy McKee Henry
Cover Photo by Betsy McKee Henry
Library of Congress Card Number - pending
the zen mama's book of quotes:
a collection of thoughts and wisdom throughout the ages/
Betsy McKee Henry
ISBN 1453752900 1st Edition
EAN 13 9781453752906

This book is dedicated to:

JOHN

Thanks for everything!

The secret of a happy marriage is finding the right person. You know they're right if you love to be with them all of the time.

~JULIA CHILD

Your friend is your needs answered.

~KHALIL GIBRAN

*Lives of great men
all remind us
We can make
our lives sublime,
And, departing,
leave behind us
Footprints on
the sands of time*

~HENRY WADSWORTH LONGFELLOW

Table of Contents

Foreword 序

All my best thoughts were stolen by the ancients.
~RALPH WALDO EMERSON

Maxim, proverb, saying, adage, dictum and aphorism. All these words describe a good quote. All cultures have them. Quotes have been around since before writing. Quotes reflect the poetry and philosophy of people we admire.

I have had a wonderful two years of self discovery. Writing How To Be A Zen Mama was a realization of a childhood dream of being an author. It also changed me. I became a better parent. During this process, I read many quotes and included them in my book and blog.

I've been inspired by quotes since the first quote book I received as a young girl from my aunt. Over the past few years, I've collected these quotes and put them in my first book. Quotes have introduced each blog post I've written. I always wanted to be one of those parents who had a quote ready for every situation. Yet, not unlike the punchline of a joke, I can never remember the quote when I need it! I am constantly looking up quotes and trying to remember where I wrote the one down that I wanted. I decided to put them all in one place for myself. That was an "aha" moment! My next book could be a collection of quotes.

Why do we love quotes? Quotes reaffirm, remind and put life into perspective. Quotes help us to understand ourselves. Quotes are popular sayings that often express common sense and universal truths. They often motivate us and make us think. Quotes inspire. Quotes pack a lot of wisdom into a few words. Quotes explain a purpose to life. During the last year I have read, studied these principles and tried to "practice what I've preached" and put them into action:

This book has five parts:

Letting Go Of...
As we get older, we often find ourselves letting go of the things that just aren't that important. We replace our negative feelings with more positive thoughts. In this part you will let go of:

• Worry
• Anger
• Fear
• Doubt
• Negative Thoughts

Practicing
It takes practice to put quotes into actions. Practice has many meanings. The definition of practice is: drill, learn by repetition, translating an idea into action, commit, engage in or perform. In this part, you'll learn to put to practice:

• Happiness and Positive Thought
• Kindness
• Listening and Speaking

- Mindfulness
- Laughter and Humor

Discovering Your Self

Some of us are born with self confidence. For others, it takes a lifetime to find ourselves. All of us have moments during our life where we're changing and rediscovering who we are. By accepting yourself, you need to accept your childhood, your parents or how you behave as a parent. Then, you can go on to discover what your passion is. In this part you will discover:

- Self Acceptance
- Being A Parent
- A Happy Childhood
- Creativity
- Discovering Your Passion

Embracing Life

You may like where you are in your life or you might not. In either case you must embrace the life you are living. With positive thought can come positive change. When you embrace life, you allow yourself to move forward. This will come after you let go of fear and other negative thoughts. In this part, you can embrace:

- Success and Wisdom
- Change
- Opportunity
- Going With The Flow
- Adventure

Finding Your Path

As we grow, whether you've just turned 16 years old or 80 years old, we are constantly on a path, finding ourselves and trying to understand the changing world around us. In this part, you will find:

• Peace
• Simplicity
• Gratitude
• Nature's Inspiration
• Compassion
• Unconditional Love

In the book you will find famous authors and unknowns, ancient thinkers and even a few characters from authors' imaginations. I hope that these authors can inspire you, too. These people, some alive and some long dead, have worked at life and faced the same issues we all face.

We are not human beings having spiritual experiences,
we are spiritual beings having human experiences.
~WAYNE DYER

LETTING
GO

If you can solve your problem,
then what is the need of worrying?
If you cannot solve it,
then what is the use of worrying?

~SHANTIDEVA

Letting Go

"What is letting go?" "Is letting go giving up?"

"I want to let go, but how do you do it?"

I've often had people ask me this question. This is a tough philosophy to describe. Letting go is admitting to yourself that you no longer need to hold on to a problem that has been causing you pain in your life, whether it's a person, a recurring thought, or a job. Many people have a lot of emotions to let go. We need to let go of worry, doubt, fear, anger and negative thoughts.

As you read the following quotes, think about releasing the need to control. Simply allowing your problem to be. Acceptance and surrender of the problem so that a change, a shift can occur. Take your emotional attachment away and what is left? It is often a daunting task to let go, but often easier than holding on.

Letting go can turn to relief. You don't have to lug the baggage around anymore.

Letting Go of Worry

If you can't sleep, then get up and do something instead of lying there and worrying. It's the worry that gets you, not the loss of sleep.
~DALE CARNEGIE

I am an old man and have known a great many troubles, but most of them never happened.
~MARK TWAIN

Let us be of good cheer, remembering that the misfortunes hardest to bear are those which will never happen.
~JAMES RUSSELL LOWELL

There is only one way to happiness, and that is to cease worrying about things which are beyond the power of our will.
~EPICTETUS

Worry often gives a small thing a big shadow.

~SWEDISH PROVERB

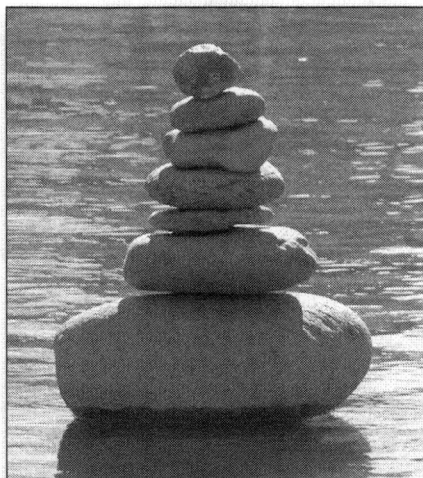

Do not anticipate trouble or worry about what may never happen. Keep in the sunlight.
~BENJAMIN FRANKLIN

How much pain they have cost us, the evils which have never happened.
~THOMAS JEFFERSON

Blessed is the person who is too busy to worry in the daytime and too sleepy to worry at night.
~AUTHOR UNKNOWN

Rule number one is, don't sweat the small stuff.
Rule number two is, it's all small stuff.
~ROBERT ELIOT

It's not a matter of letting go--you would if you could.
Instead of "Let it go," we should probably say "Let it be."
~JON KABAT-ZINN

Letting Go of Doubt

There is nothing more dreadful than the habit of doubt. Doubt separates people. It is the poison that disintegrates friendships and breaks up pleasant relationships. It is a thorn that irritates and hurts. It is a sword that kills.
~BUDDHA

Sometimes, looking back, we wonder why we are doing all this, and sometimes we think, why not?
~TRUNGPA RINPOCHE

Our doubts are traitors and make us lose the good we oft might win, by fearing to attempt.
~WILLIAM SHAKESPEARE

Doubt is the beginning not the end of wisdom.
~PROVERB

Dubito ergo cogito; cogito ergo sum.
(I doubt, therefore I think; I think therefore I am)
~RENE DESCARTES

信心

"Faith"

Doubt is a pain too lonely
to know that faith is his
twin brother.

~KHALIL GIBRAN

Faith keeps many doubts in her pay. If I could not doubt, I should not believe.
~HENRY DAVID THOREAU

Faith and doubt both are needed -- not as antagonists, but working side by side to take us around the unknown curve.
~LILLIAN SMITH

11

Faith given back to us after a night of doubt is a stronger thing, and far more valuable to us than faith that has never been tested.

~ELIZABETH GOUGE

Letting Go of Anger

If you kick a stone in anger, you'll hurt your own foot.

~KOREAN PROVERB

Life is too short to hold a grudge, also too long.
~ROBERT BRAULT

Keep your words soft and tender because tomorrow
you may have to eat them.
~AUTHOR UNKNOWN

Holding on to anger is like grasping a hot coal with
the intent of throwing it at someone else; you are the
one who gets burned.
~BUDDHA

For every minute you are angry you lose sixty seconds
of happiness.
~RALPH WALDO EMERSON

Don't hold on to anger, hurt or pain. They steal your energy and keep you from love.
~LEO BUSCAGLIA

If your heart is a volcano, how shall you expect flowers to bloom?
~KAHLIL GIBRAN

If you are patient in one moment of anger, you will escape a hundred days of sorrow.

~CHINESE PROVERB

Letting Go of Fear

I have learned to live each day as it comes, and not to borrow trouble by dreading tomorrow. It is the dark menace of the future that makes cowards of us.
~DOROTHY DAY

Nothing in life is to be feared. It is only to be understood.
~MARIE CURIE

He who fears something gives it power over him.
~MOORISH PROVERB

I have accepted fear as a part of life -- specifically the fear of change...I have gone ahead despite the pounding in the heart that says: turn back.
~ERICA JONG

Don't let the fear of the time it will take to accomplish something stand in the way of your doing it. The time will pass anyway; we might just as well put that passing time to the best possible use.
~EARL NIGHTINGALE

Fear and courage are brothers.

~PROVERB

Letting Go of
Negative Thought

One can overcome the forces of negative emotions,
like anger and hatred, by cultivating their
counterforces, like love and compassion.
~DALAI LAMA

Change your thoughts, and you change your world.
~NORMAN VINCENT PEALE

True salvation is freedom from negativity, and above
all, from past and future as a psychological need.
~ECKHART TOLLE

Be vigilant; guard your mind against negative thoughts.
~BUDDHA

When negative feelings are suppressed positive feelings
become suppressed as well, and love dies.
~JOHN GRAY

A man is but the product of his thoughts. What he thinks, he becomes.
~MAHATMA GANDHI

Every thought is a seed. If you plant crab apples, don't count on harvesting Golden Delicious.
~BILL MEYER

Whenever a negative thought concerning your personal power comes to mind, deliberately voice a positive one to cancel it out.
~NORMAN VINCENT PEALE

Fear less, hope more; Eat less, chew more; Whine less, breathe more; Talk less, say more; Love more, and all good things will be yours.
~SWEDISH PROVERB

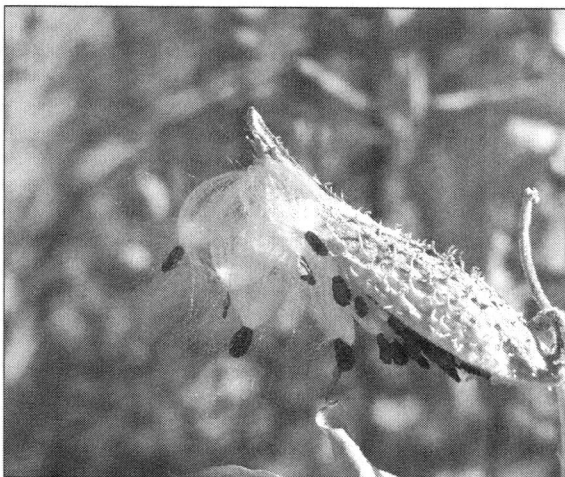

To Let Go

To Let Go is not to care for,
but to care about.
To Let Go is not to fix, but to be supportive.
To Let Go is not to judge,
but to allow another to be a human being.
To Let Go is not to be in the middle of
arranging all outcomes,
but to allow others to effect
their own destinies.
To Let Go is not to be protective,
but to permit others to face reality.
To Let Go is to fear less, and to love more.

~AUTHOR UNKNOWN

In deep self-acceptance grows a compassionate understanding. As one Zen master said when I asked if he ever gets angry, "Of course I get angry, but then a few minutes later I say to myself, 'What's the use of this', and I let it go."

~JACK KORNFIELD

PRACTICING

Practice is the best of all instructors.

~PUBLILIUS SYRUS

An ounce of practice is worth

more than tons of preaching.

~MAHATMA GANDHI

Nobody in life gets exactly what they thought they were going to get. But if you work really hard, and you're kind, amazing things will happen.

~Conan O'Brien

Practice

Now that you've let go of negative habits, it is time to practice the positive.

It takes practice to put quotes into actions. Practice has many meanings. The definition of practice is: drill, learn by repetition, translating an idea into action, commit, engage in or perform.

Anyone who has played sports can tell you that when the team practices, they discover their mistakes. When you discover your mistakes, you can change them and become a winning team.

In the same way, cultivating happiness, kindness, mindfulness, listening, speaking, laughter and humor takes practice. Just as negative thoughts can become habits, these positive practices can become habits.

Are you practicing positive habits?

Happiness and Positive Thought

Attitudes are contagious. Are yours worth catching?
~DENNIS AND WENDY MANNERING

All that we are is the result of what we have thought.
The mind is everything. What we think we become.
~BUDDHA

I had the blues because I had no shoes until upon the
street, I met a man who had no feet.
~ANCIENT PERSIAN SAYING

The foolish man seeks happiness in the distance.
The wise man grows it under his feet.
~JAMES OPPENHEIM

Happiness is like a butterfly which, when pursued, is always beyond our grasp, but, if you will sit down quietly, may alight upon you.

~NATHANIEL HAWTHORNE

In the depth of winter I finally learned that there was in me an invincible summer.

~ALBERT CAMUS

Man is fond of counting his troubles, but he does not count his joys. If he counted them up as he ought to, he would see that every lot has enough happiness provided for it.

~FYODOR DOSTOEVSKY

Happiness often sneaks in through a door you didn't know you left open.

~JOHN BARRYMORE

Joy is a flower that blooms when you do.

~AUTHOR UNKNOWN

Once you replace negative thoughts with positive ones, you'll start having positive results.

~WILLIE NELSON

幸福

"Happiness"

*Sometimes your joy
is the source of your smile,
but sometimes your smile
can be the source of your joy.*

~THICH NHAT HANH

Since the house is on fire let us warm ourselves.
~ITALIAN PROVERB

If you concentrate on finding whatever is good in every situation, you will discover that your life will suddenly be filled with gratitude, a feeling that nurtures the soul.
~RABBI HAROLD KUSHNER

A pessimist sees the difficulty in every opportunity; an optimist sees the opportunity in every difficulty.
~WINSTON CHURCHILL

Kindness

Be kind whenever possible. It is always possible.
~THE DALAI LAMA

Do unto others as you would have them do unto you.
~MATTHEW 7:12

Kindness in words creates confidence, kindness in thinking creates profoundness, kindness in feeling creates love.
~LAO TZU

Sometimes, all it takes is one kind word to nourish another person. Think of the ripple effect that can be created when we nourish someone. One kind empathetic word has a wonderful way of turning into many.
~MISTER (FRED) ROGERS

My religion is very simple.
My religion is kindness.

~DALAI LAMA

A kind word is like a
Spring day.

~RUSSIAN PROVERB

No act of kindness, no matter how small, is ever wasted.
~AESOP

I expect to pass through this world but once; any good thing therefore that I can do, or any kindness that I can show to any fellow creature, let me do it now; let me not defer or neglect it, for I shall not pass this way again.
~ETTIENE DE GRELLET

Kindness should become the natural way of life, not the exception.
~BUDDHA

Wherever there is a human being, there is an opportunity for a kindness.
~SENECA

You cannot do a kindness too soon, for you never know how soon it will be too late.
~RALPH WALDO EMERSON

Be kind, for everyone you meet is fighting a hard battle.
~PLATO

A bit of fragrance always clings to the hand that gives roses.

~CHINESE PROVERB

The best way to knock the chip off your neighbor's shoulder is to pat him on the back.

~AUTHOR UNKNOWN

Listening and Speaking

We have two ears and one mouth so that we can listen
twice as much as we speak.
~EPICTETUS

Courage is what it takes to stand up and speak;
courage is also what it takes to sit down and listen.
~WINSTON CHURCHILL

仁慈

"Kindness"

*The kindest word
in all the world
is the unkind word,
unsaid.*

~AUTHOR UNKNOWN

If you wouldn't write it and sign it, don't say it.
~EARL WILSON

You can catch more flies with honey.
~DONALD R. HENRY

Too often we underestimate the power of a touch,
a smile, a kind word, a listening ear, an honest
compliment, or the smallest act of caring,
all of which have the potential to turn a life around.
~LEO BUSCAGLIA

He bites his tongue who speaks in haste.
~TURKISH PROVERB

Listen or thy tongue will keep thee deaf.
~NATIVE AMERICAN INDIAN PROVERB

Mindfulness

A man who dares to waste one hour of time has not discovered the value of life.
~CHARLES DARWIN

Do not dwell in the past, do not dream of the future, concentrate the mind on the present moment.
~BUDDHA

The future depends on what we do in the present.
~MAHATMA GHANDI

At first, I saw mountains as mountains and rivers as rivers. Then, I saw mountains were not mountains and rivers were not rivers. Finally, I see mountains again as mountains, and rivers again as rivers.
~ZEN PROVERB

Every Spring is the only Spring -
a perpetual astonishment.

~ELLIS PETERS

The most precious gift we can
offer others is our presence.
When mindfulness embraces
those we love, they will
bloom like flowers.

~THICH NHAT HANH

When walking, walk. When eating, eat.
~ZEN PROVERB

Winning is important to me, but what brings me real joy is the experience of being fully engaged in whatever I'm doing.
~PHIL JACKSON

And remember, no matter where you go, there you are.
~CONFUCIUS

If you surrender completely to the moments as they pass, you live more richly those moments.
~ANNE MORROW LINDBERGH

You must live in the present, launch yourself on every wave, find your eternity in each moment.
~HENRY DAVID THOREAU

Every day is my best day; this is my life; I am not going to have this moment again.
~BERNIE SIEGEL

Cultivating a generous spirit starts with mindfulness. Mindfulness, simply stated, means paying attention to what is actually happening; it's about what is really going on.
~NELL NEWMAN

No snowflake falls in an inappropriate place.
~ZEN PROVERB

*Mindfulness is mirror-thought.
It reflects only what is presently
happening and in exactly
the way it is happening.
Mindfulness is non-judgmental
observation. It is that ability of
the mind to observe without
criticism. Being aware and being
awake to the present moment.*

~THICH NHAN HANH

Laughter and Humor

Today, give a stranger one of your smiles. It might be the only sunshine he sees all day.
~QUOTED IN THE MOVIE: P.S. I LOVE YOU

Laughter is brightest where food is best.
~IRISH PROVERB

Birthdays are good for you. Statistics show that the people who have the most live the longest.
~FATHER LARRY LORENZONI

Take time to laugh -- it is the music of the soul.
~OLD ENGLISH PRAYER

Humor is the great thing, the saving thing. The minute it crops up, all our irritation and resentments slip away, and a sunny spirit takes their place.
~MARK TWAIN

A good laugh and a long sleep are the best cures in the doctor's book.

~IRISH PROVERB

Every time you smile at someone, it is an action of love, a gift to that person, a beautiful thing.

~MOTHER TERESA

It is impossible for you to be angry and laugh at the same time. Anger and laughter are mutually exclusive and you have the power to choose either.

~WAYNE DYER

We cannot really love someone with whom we never laugh.

~ALICE REPPLIER

Life is like a mirror, we get the best results when we smile at it.

~AUTHOR UNKNOWN

Life is far too important to be taken seriously.

~OSCAR WILDE

*Find something you're
passionate about and keep
tremendously interested in it.*

~JULIA CHILD

THE JOURNEY OF SELF DISCOVERY

When the student is ready,
the teacher will appear.

~ZEN PROVERB

*Life is not having and getting,
but being and becoming.*

~MATTHEW ARNOLD

Your True Self

Discovering ourselves starts from the time we first turn over as babies and does not stop until we die. There is never a moment that we're finished with growing and changing. It starts with self acceptance which can be a very difficult concept in our pop culture.

Part of our journey is being a parent. Many emotions surround being a parent. Is there anything more wonderful than having a baby? Is there anything more challenging than having a child? These quotes might make you smile and realize that we're all in the same boat. When we become parents we re-experience our own childhood for good or bad. We are all children of parents as well. We can be more compassionate to our own parents and remember what they went through. As a parent, we can treasure our children and help them on their own path to discovering themselves. By giving a child a happy childhood, we can make their adulthood "baggageless".

On the journey of self discovery we discover our passion. It is essential to a happy life to do what we love. When you discover yourself you also discover your true creativity.

Self Acceptance

They cannot take away our self-respect if we do not give it to them.

~MAHATMA GANDHI

If you want to be respected by others, the great thing is to respect yourself. Only by that, only by self respect, will you compel others to respect you.
~FYODOR DOSTOEVSKY

The best day of your life is the one on which you decide your life is your own. No apologies or excuses. No one to lean on, rely on, or blame. The gift is yours – it is an amazing journey – and you alone are responsible for the quality of it. This is the day your life really begins.
~BOB MOAWAD

It is not easy to find happiness in ourselves, and it is not possible to find it elsewhere.
~AGNES REPPLIER

To love oneself is the beginning of a life-long romance.
~OSCAR WILDE

Always be a first-rate version of yourself, instead of a second-rate version of somebody else.
~JUDY GARLAND

No one can make you feel inferior without your consent.
~ELEANOR ROOSEVELT

To free us from the expectations of others, to give us back to ourselves -- there lies the great, singular power of self-respect.
~JOAN DIDION

A man cannot be comfortable without his own approval.
~MARK TWAIN

God, grant me the serenity to accept the things I cannot change, the courage to change the things I can, and the wisdom to know the difference.
~REINHOLD NIEBUHR

Everything that irritates us about others can lead us to an understanding of ourselves.
~CARL GUSTAVE JUNG

The sculptor produces the beautiful statue by chipping away such parts of the marble block as are not needed-it is a process of elimination.

~ELBERT HUBBARD

Being a Parent

This is part of the essence of motherhood, watching your kid grow into her own person and not being able to do anything about it. Otherwise children would be nothing more than pets.
~HEATHER ARMSTRONG

The world is full of women blindsided by the unceasing demands of motherhood, still flabbergasted by how a job can be terrific and torturous.
~ANNA QUINDLEN

The central struggle of parenthood is to let our hopes for our children outweigh our fears.
~ELLEN GOODMAN

I'd like to be the ideal mother, but I'm too busy raising my kids.
~UNKNOWN

Part of the fun of being a parent is acting like you
don't know anything, so your kids can tell you
everything they think they know.
~JOHN H. HENRY

A parent's love is whole no matter how many times divided.
~ROBERT BRAULT

I hope you're proud of yourself for the times you've
said yes, when all it meant was extra work for you and
was seemingly only helpful to someone else.
~MISTER (FRED) ROGERS

You need to be aware of what others are doing,
applaud their efforts, acknowledge their successes, and
encourage them in their pursuits. When we all help
one another, everybody wins.
~JIM STOVALL

I think it's the great thing about having kids. They
have interests that you might not have, and it opens
your horizons.
~ROBERT MARTIN

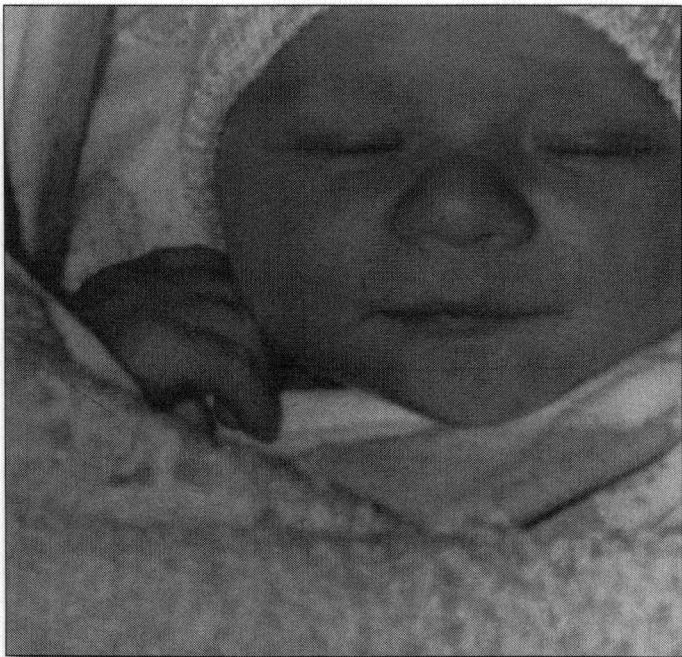

The moment a child is born, the mother is also born. The woman existed, but the mother, never. A mother is something new.

~RAJNEESH

I have found the best way to give advice to your children is to find out what they want and then advise them to do it.

~HARRY S TRUMAN

While we try to teach our children all about life, our children teach us what life is all about.

~ANGELA SCHWINDT

Your children are not your children. They are the sons and daughters of Life's longing for itself. They came through you but not from you and though they are with you yet they belong not to you.

~KAHLIL GIBRAN

An aware parent loves all children he or she meets and interacts with -- for you are a caretaker for those moments in time.

~DOC CHILDRE

A Happy Childhood

Never fear spoiling children by making them too
happy. Happiness is the atmosphere in which all good
affections grow.
~THOMAS BRAY

If a child is to keep his inborn sense of wonder, he
needs the companionship of at least one adult who
can share it.
~RACHEL CARSON

The child supplies the power but the parents have to
do the steering.
~BENJAMIN SPOCK

Children need love, especially when they do not
deserve it.
~HAROLD HULBERT

A child's life is like a piece of paper on which every person leaves a mark.

~CHINESE PROVERB

We worry about what a child will become tomorrow, yet we forget that he is someone today.

~STACIA TAUSCHER

If you've had a happy childhood, no one can ever take that away. If you've had an unhappy childhood, you'll search for it the rest of your life. Give your children a happy childhood. Treasure your children.

~THE ZEN MAMA

Please give me some good advice in your next letter. I promise not to follow it.

~EDNA ST. VINCENT MILLAY

In youth we learn; in age we understand.
~MARIE EBNER-ESCHENBACH

If you carry your childhood with you, you never become older.
~TOM STOPPARD

Children will not remember you for the material things you provided but for the feeling that you cherished them.
~RICHARD L. EVANS

Creativity and Imagination

It's not what you look at that matters, it's what you see.
~HENRY DAVID THOREAU

Imagination disposes of everything; it creates beauty, justice, and happiness, which is everything in this world.
~PASCAL

Imagination is more important than knowledge. For knowledge is limited to all we now know and understand, while imagination embraces the entire world, and all there ever will be to know and understand.
~ALBERT EINSTEIN

The creative is the place where no one else has ever been. You have to leave the city of your comfort and go into the wilderness of your intuition. What you'll discover will be wonderful. What you'll discover is yourself.
~ALAN ALDA

Creativity is inventing, experimenting, growing, taking risks, breaking rules, making mistakes, and having fun.
~MARY LOU COOK

To be creative means to be in love with life. You can be creative only if you love life enough that you want to enhance its beauty, you want to bring a little more music to it, a little more poetry to it, a little more dance to it.
~OSHO

An artist paints, dances, draws, writes, designs, or acts at the expanding edge of consciousness. We press into the unknown rather than the known. This makes life lovely and lively.
~JULIA CAMERON

Every child is an artist. The problem is how to remain an artist once he grows up.
~PABLO PICASSO

Creativity is allowing yourself to make mistakes. Art is knowing which ones to keep.
~SCOTT ADAMS

A rock pile ceases to be a rock pile the moment a single man contemplates it, bearing within him the image of a cathedral.

~ANTOINE DE SAINT-EXUPÉRY

Discovering Your Passion and Purpose

What you're seeking is seeking you.

~RUMI

The world needs dreamers and the world needs doers.
But above all, the world needs dreamers who do.

~SARAH BAN BREATHNACH

It is never too late to be what you might have been.

~GEORGE ELIOT

If we all did the things we are capable of doing,
we would literally astound ourselves.

~THOMAS A. EDISON

Do what you love and the money will follow.
~MARSHA SINETAR

First say to yourself what you would be, and then do what you have to do.
~EPICTETUS

Chase down your passion like it's the last bus of the night.
~TERRI GUILLEMETS

Doing what you love is the cornerstone of having abundance in your life.
~WAYNE DYER

All our dreams can come true -- if we have the courage to pursue them.
~WALT DISNEY

Far and away the best prize that life offers is the chance to work hard at work worth doing.
~THEODORE ROOSEVELT

If you want to be happy
for a day, go on a picnic.
If you want to be happy
for a week, go on a vacation.
If you want to be happy
for a year, inherit wealth.
If you want to be happy
for a lifetime, do the work
that you love.

~AUTHOR UNKNOWN

I enjoy my work so much that I have to be pulled away from my work into leisure.

~RALPH NADER

Without work, all life goes rotten. But when work is soulless, life stifles and dies.

~ALBERT CAMUS

Work is love made visible. And if you cannot work with love but only with distaste, it is better that you should leave your work and sit at the gate of the temple and take alms of those who work with joy.

~KAHLIL GIBRAN

Your work is to discover your world and then with all your heart give yourself to it.

~BUDDHA

热情

"Passion"

I am always doing things I can't do. That is how I get to do them.

~PABLO PICASSO

In response to those who say to stop dreaming and face reality, I say keep dreaming and make reality.

~KRISTIAN KAN

Follow your bliss and the universe will open doors where there were only walls.

~JOSEPH CAMPBELL

EMBRACING
LIFE

When written in Chinese, the word "crisis" is composed of two characters. One represents danger and the other represents opportunity.

~JOHN F. KENNEDY

Most folks are about as happy as they make up their minds to be.

~ABRAHAM LINCOLN

Embracing Life

"Dost thou love life?" asked Benjamin Franklin. Some of us find life easy. Others constantly battle life. Do you just let life happen to you? Or do you go for it! If you embrace what is around you, flow as if going down a river instead of fighting upstream and against the current, life will be easier for you.

What does it mean to embrace life? It means to trust that life is happening to you the way it should. It is embracing life's opportunities instead of waiting. It is taking a second look at change and seeing the value in it. It's looking at the true meaning of success and seeing money doesn't always have a lot to do with it.

Life should also be thought of as an adventure whether you're finding it in your own backyard or traveling all over the world.

Embracing life is realizing that there's no looking back, no regrets, no shouldas. It is enjoying the moment and looking forward!

Success and Wisdom

To laugh often and much;
To win the respect of intelligent
people and the affection
of children;
To earn the appreciation of honest
critics and endure the betrayal
of false friends;
To appreciate beauty, to find
the best in others;
To leave the world a bit better,
whether by a healthy child,
a garden patch or a redeemed
social condition;
To know even one life has
breathed easier because
you have lived.
This is to have succeeded.

~RALPH WALDO EMERSON

Je ne regrette rien. (I regret nothing)
~SUNG BY EDITH PIAFF

Great spirits have always encountered violent
opposition from mediocre minds.
~ALBERT EINSTEIN

Wisdom is knowing what to do next; virtue is doing it.
~DAVID STAR JORDAN

By three methods we may learn wisdom:
First, by reflection, which is noblest;
Second, by imitation, which is easiest;
and third by experience, which is the bitterest.
~CONFUCIUS

The farther you go, the less you know.
~LAO TZU

The teacher who is indeed wise does not bid you to enter the house of his wisdom but rather leads you to the threshold of your mind.

~Kahlil Gibran

Early to bed and early to rise, makes a man healthy, wealthy and wise.

~Benjamin Franklin

You can tell whether a man is clever by his answers. You can tell whether a man is wise by his questions.

~Naguib Mahfouz

Knowledge comes, but wisdom lingers.

~Alfred Lord Tennyson

Before we acquire great power, we must acquire wisdom to use it well.

~Ralph Waldo Emerson

Change

If you change the way you look at things, the things you look at change.

~WAYNE DYER

A life without change is not a life; it is a stagnant pool. To change your mind frivolously is a cop-out. To change your mind under the direction of the wisdom of the heart is a brush stroke on the masterpiece you are delivering to the world.

~ALAN COHEN

Never be afraid to try something new. Remember, amateurs built the ark. Professionals built the Titanic.

~ANONYMOUS

If you don't like something, change it; if you can't change it, change the way you think about it.

~MARY ENGELBREIT

Things don't change. You change your way of looking, that's all.

~CARLOS CASTENEDA

You must be the change you wish to see in the world.

~MAHATMA GHANDI

All things change, nothing is extinguished. There is nothing in the whole world which is permanent. Everything flows onward; all things are brought into being with a changing nature; the ages themselves glide by in constant movement.

~OVID

They must often change, who would be constant in happiness or wisdom.

~CONFUCIUS

Change always comes bearing gifts.

~PRICE PRITCHETT

You can never step into the same river; for new waters are always flowing on to you.

~HERACLITUS OF EPHESUS

God grant me the serenity to accept the people I cannot change, the courage to change the one I can, and the wisdom to know it's me.

~AUTHOR UNKNOWN

If nothing ever changed,
there'd be no butterflies.

~AUTHOR UNKNOWN

Opportunity

There is no education like adversity.
~DISRAELI

There are no mistakes, no coincidences.
All events are blessings given to us to learn from.
~ELIZABETH KUBLER-ROSS

The road to success is always under construction.
~LILY TOMLIN

A pessimist sees the difficulty in every opportunity;
an optimist sees the opportunity in every difficulty.
~WINSTON CHURCHILL

Why always "not yet"? Do flowers in spring say "not yet"?
~NORMAN DOUGLAS

Three Rules of Work:
Out of clutter find simplicity;
From discord find harmony;
In the middle of difficulty
lies opportunity.

~ALBERT EINSTEIN

It is our choices...that show what we truly are,
far more than our abilities.

~ALBUS DUMBLEDORE

Opportunity is missed by most people because it is
dressed in overalls and looks like work.

~THOMAS EDISON

Though no one can go back and make a brand new
start, anyone can start from now and make a brand
new ending.

~AUTHOR UNKNOWN

Anyone who has never made a mistake has never tried anything new.

~ALBERT EINSTEIN

Never Give Up!

~ANYONE WHO'S EVER SUCCEEDED

When one door closes, another opens: but we often look so long and so regretfully upon the closed door that we do not see the one which has opened for us.

~ALEXANDER GRAHAM BELL

A successful person is one who can lay a firm foundation with the bricks that others throw at him or her.

~DAVID BRINKLEY

Recognizing Flow

By banishing doubt and trusting your intuitive feelings, you clear a space for the power of intention to flow through.
~WAYNE DYER

Life is a series of natural and spontaneous changes. Don't resist them -- that only creates sorrow. Let reality be reality. Let things flow naturally forward in whatever way they like.
~LAO-TZU

Flow with whatever is happening and let your mind be free. Stay centered by accepting whatever you are doing. This is the ultimate.
~CHUANG TZU

Everything flows and nothing abides, everything gives way and nothing stays fixed.
~HERACLITUS

Row, Row, Row Your Boat
Gently Down The Stream
Merrily, Merrily, Merrily Merrily
Life is but a dream.
~CHILDHOOD SONG

Serendipity is looking in a haystack for a needle and discovering a farmer's daughter.
~JULIUS COMROE, JR.

Seek not the things which happen should happen as you wish; but wish the things which happened to be as they are and you will have a tranquil flow of life.
~EPICTETUS

There are no mistakes, no coincidences. All events are blessings given to us to learn from.
~ELIZABETH KUBLER ROSS

Be like the fountain
that overflows, not like the
cistern that merely contains.

~ PAULO COELHO

Discovering Adventure

*Two roads diverged
in a wood, and I,
I took the one
less traveled by,
And that has made
all the difference.*

~ROBERT FROST

*Do not go where the path may
lead, go instead where there is
no path and leave a trail.*

~RALPH WALDO EMERSON

Twenty years from now you will be more disappointed by the things you didn't do than by the ones you did do. So throw off the bowlines, sail away from the safe harbor. Catch the trade winds in your sails. Explore. Dream. Discover.

~MARK TWAIN

The World is a book, and those who do not travel read only a page.

~ST. AUGUSTINE

We live in a wonderful world that is full of beauty, charm and adventure. There is no end to the adventures we can have if only we seek them with our eyes open.

~JAWAHARIAL NEHRU

Life is either a daring adventure, or nothing.

~HELEN KELLER

You don't get to choose how you're going to die. Or when. You can only decide how you're going to live. Now.

~JOAN BAEZ

FOLLOW YOUR PATH

I have just three things to teach:
simplicity, patience, compassion.
These three are your greatest treasures.

~LAO TZU

Following Your Path

There is a point in everyone's life when spirituality takes on meaning. For some it happens early in life. For others it could take place as death nears. For most of us, spirituality finds us somewhere in the middle of life.

Does it matter whether you are Christian, Muslim, Jewish, Hindu or have your own brand of spirituality? All religions have universal truths. Even if you don't believe in God, there is a spirituality that you can find in life that can be followed.

Spirituality often comes into our lives after a meaningful experience. Loneliness, divorce or the death of a loved one can bring it. Or a positive experience like working among children, or the poor. Being in love or having a child can connect you to a higher purpose.

Harmony, balance, waking up to a sense of higher purpose rather than just going through the motions of life, is finding spirituality. So, go look for inspiration, find your own path and follow it!

Peace

Imagine all the people living life in peace. You may say I'm a dreamer, but I'm not the only one. I hope someday you'll join us, and the world will be as one.

~JOHN LENNON

Peace is every step.
The shining red sun is my heart.
Each flower smiles with me.
How green, how fresh
all that grows.
How cool the wind that blows.
It turns the endless path to joy.

~THICT NHAT HAHN

We can never obtain peace in the outer world
until we make peace with ourselves.

~DALAI LAMA

Peace. It does not mean to be in a place where there is
no noise, trouble or hard work. It means to be in the
midst of those things, and still be calm in your heart.

~UNKNOWN

Peace comes from within.
Do not seek it without.

~BUDDHA

An eye for eye only ends up making the whole world
blind.

~MAHATMA GANDHI

Let there be peace on earth
And let it begin with me.

~SEYMOUR MILLER & JILL JACKSON

Finding Simplicity

Our life is frittered away by detail...Simplify, simplify, simplify!...Simplicity of life and elevation of purpose.
~HENRY DAVID THOREAU

Have nothing in your houses that you do not know to be useful or believe to be beautiful.
~WILLIAM MORRIS

Simplicity is the ultimate sophistication.
~LEONARDO DaVINCI

Let us learn to live simply, so that others may simply live.
~MAHATMA GANDHI

Who is rich? He who rejoices in his portion.
~THE TALMUD

Be content with what you have,
rejoice in the way things are.
When you realize there is
nothing lacking, the whole
world belongs to you.

~LAO TZU

Eat when you're hungry.
Drink when you're thirsty.
Sleep when you're tired.

~BUDDHIST PROVERB

I believe that a simple and unassuming manner of life is best for everyone, best both for the body and the mind.
~ALBERT EINSTEIN

Simplicity and repose are the qualities that measure the true value of any work of art.
~FRANK LLOYD WRIGHT

Fear less, hope more; eat less, chew more; whine less, breathe more; talk less, say more; love more, and all good things will be yours.
~SWEDISH PROVERB

I am beginning to learn that it is the sweet, simple things in life which are the real ones after all.
~LAURA INGALLS WILDER

Simplicity is making the journey of this life with just baggage enough.
~AUTHOR UNKNOWN

Life is really simple, but we insist on making it complicated.
~CONFUCIUS

Gratitude

There are only two ways to live your life. One is as though nothing is a miracle. The other is as though everything is a miracle.
~ALBERT EINSTEIN

You have no cause for anything but gratitude and joy.
~THE BUDDHA

Let us be grateful to people who make us happy; they are the charming gardeners who make our souls blossom.
~MARCEL PROUST

God gave you a gift of 86,400 seconds today. Have you used one to say "thank you?"
~WILLIAM A. WARD

Gratitude is the best attitude.
~AUTHOR UNKNOWN

*At times our own light goes out
and is rekindled by a spark
from another person.
Each of us has cause to think
with deep gratitude of those who
have lighted the flame within us.*

~ALBERT SCHWEITZER

You simply will not be the same person two months from now after consciously giving thanks each day for the abundance that exists in your life. And you will have set in motion an ancient spiritual law: the more you have and are grateful for, the more will be given you.

~SARAH BAN BREATHNACH

When eating bamboo sprouts, remember the man who planted them.

~CHINESE PROVERB

Feeling gratitude and not expressing it is like wrapping a present and not giving it.

~WILLIAM ARTHUR WARD

Take full account of the excellencies which you possess, and in gratitude remember how you would hanker after them, if you had them not.

~MARCUS AURELIUS

Feeling grateful or appreciative of someone or something in your life actually attracts more of the things that you appreciate and value into your life.

~CHRISTIANE NORTHRUP

Gratitude is riches. Complaint is poverty.
~DORIS DAY

Let us rise up and be thankful, for if we didn't learn a lot today, at least we learned a little, and if we didn't learn a little, at least we didn't get sick, and if we got sick, at least we didn't die; so, let us all be thankful.
~BUDDHA

No one is as capable of gratitude as one who has emerged from the kingdom of night.
~ELIE WIESEL

Reflect upon your present blessings, of which every man has plenty; not on your past misfortunes of which all men have some.
~CHARLES DICKENS

For each new morning with its light,
For rest and shelter of the night,
For health and food,
for love and friends,
Feeling gratitude
and not expressing it is
like wrapping a present
and not giving it.

~WILLIAM ARTHUR WARD

Nature's Inspiration

Heaven is under our feet, as well as over our heads.
~HENRY DAVID THOREAU

When I admire the wonder of a sunset or the beauty of the moon, my soul expands in worship of the Creator.
~MAHATMA GANDHI

Nature is pleased with simplicity.
~ISAAC NEWTON

Adopt the pace of nature: her secret is patience.
~RALPH WALDO EMERSON

God writes the gospel not in the Bible alone, but on trees and flowers and clouds and stars.
~MARTIN LUTHER

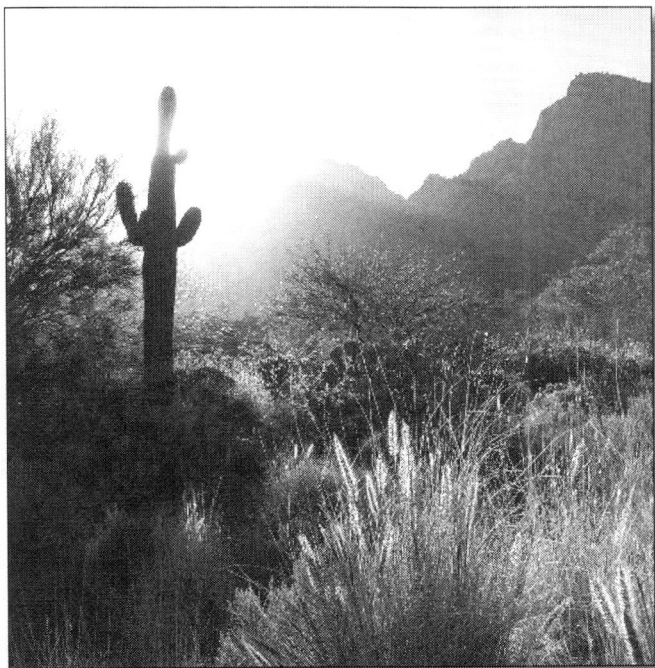

*What makes the desert
beautiful is that somewhere
it hides a well.*

~ANTOINE DE SAINT-EXUPERY

Those who dwell among the beauties and mysteries of
the earth are never alone or weary of life.
~RACHEL CARSON

You are a child of the universe, no less than the trees
and the stars; you have a right to be here.
~DESIDERATA

The richness I achieve comes from Nature,
the source of my inspiration.
~CLAUDE MONET

Is it so small a thing
To have enjoyed the sun,
To have lived light in the spring,
To have loved, to have thought, to have done?
~MATTHEW ARNOLD

Turn your face to the sun and the shadows fall behind you.
~MAORI PROVERB

The best remedy for those who are afraid, lonely or unhappy is to go outside, somewhere where they can be quiet, alone with the heavens, nature and God. Because only then does one feel that all is as it should be and that God wishes to see people happy, amidst the simple beauty of nature. I firmly believe that nature brings solace in all troubles.
~ANNE FRANK

The sun, with all those planets revolving around it and dependent on it, can still ripen a bunch of grapes as if it had nothing else in the universe to do.
~GALILEO

Whoever loves and understands a garden will find contentment within.
~CHINESE PROVERB

To forget how to dig the earth and to tend the soil is to forget ourselves.
~GANDHI

*Climb the mountains and get
their good tidings. Nature's
peace will flow into you as
sunshine flows into trees.
The winds will blow their own
freshness into you, and the
storms their energy, while cares
will drop off like autumn leaves.*

~JOHN MUIR

Lose yourself in nature and find peace.
~RALPH WALDO EMERSON

Study nature, love nature, stay close to nature.
It will never fail you.
~FRANK LLOYD WRIGHT

Those who contemplate the beauty of the earth find
reserves of strength that will endure as long as life lasts.
~RACHEL CARSON

A society grows great when old men plant trees
whose shade they know they shall never sit in.
~GREEK PROVERB

I went to the woods because I wished to live
deliberately, to front only the essential facts of life, and
see if I could not learn what it had to teach, and not,
when I came to die, discover that I had not lived.
~HENRY DAVID THOREAU

**Nature does not hurry,
yet everything is accomplished.**

~LAO TZU

Compassion

If you light a lamp for somebody, it will also brighten your own path.
~BUDDHA

If you want others to be happy, practice compassion. If you want to be happy, practice compassion.
~DALAI LAMA

Happiness comes when your work and words are of benefit to yourself and others.
~BUDDHA

Those who bring sunshine to the lives of others cannot keep it from themselves.
~JAMES M. BARRIE

If you want to know what a man's like, take a good look at how he treats his inferiors, not his equals.
~J.K. ROWLING

Love and compassion are necessities, not luxuries.
Without them humanity cannot survive.
~DALAI LAMA

Never doubt that a small group of thoughtful,
committed people can change the world...it is the only
thing that ever has.
~MARGARET MEADE

The first person served by service is the server.
~SEAN PENN

There is a destiny that makes us brothers:
none goes his way alone,
All that we send into the lives of others
comes back into our own.
~EDWIN MARKHAM

Some people, like flowers,
give pleasure, just by being.

~RALPH WALDO EMERSON

Unconditional Love

Love…What is love? Love is to love someone for who they are, who they were, and who they will be.
~CHRIS MOORE

Keep love in your heart. A life without it is like a sunless garden when the flowers are dead. The consciousness of loving and being loved brings a warmth and richness to life that nothing else can bring.
~OSCAR WILDE

It is only with the heart that one can see rightly; what is essential is invisible to the eye.
~ANTOINE DE SAINT EXUPÉRY

And ever has it been known that love knows not its own depth until the hour of separation.
~KAHLIL GIBRAN

Love is the only force capable of transforming an enemy into a friend.

~MARTIN LUTHER KING

Being deeply loved by someone gives you strength, while loving someone deeply gives you courage.

~LAO TZU

The ultimate lesson all of us have to learn is unconditional love, which includes not only others but ourselves as well.

~ELISABETH KUBLER-ROSS

Love is what's in the room with you at Christmas if you stop opening presents and listen.

~AUTHOR UNKNOWN, ATTRIBUTED TO A 7-YEAR-OLD NAMED BOBBY

Wake at dawn with a winged heart and give thanks for another day of loving.

~KAHLIL GIBRAN

*Whatever they grow up to be,
they are still our children,
and the one most important
of all the things we can give to
them is unconditional love.
Not a love that depends on
anything at all except that
they are our children.*

~ROSALEEN DICKSON

The Authors
of the Quotes

Here are most of the authors of
the Zen Mama's Quote Book:

a

Scott Adams (1957) is the American creator of the Dilbert comic strip and the author of several nonfiction works.

Aesop (620 – 564 BC) was a Greek slave known for his fables. He was most likely freed.

Alan Alda (1936) is an American actor, director and screen-writer.

Aristotle (384 BC – 322 BC) was an ancient Greek philosopher. He was a student of Plato and teacher of Alexander the Great.

Heather B. Armstrong (1975) is a blogger from Salt Lake City who writes under the name of Dooce.

Matthew Arnold (1822 – 1888) was an English poet and cultural critic who worked as an inspector of schools.

St. Augustine (354 – 430), also known as Augustine of Hippo. He was a Catholic Bishop who lived in Roman Africa. His writings helped to develop the early church.

Marcus Aurelius (121 – 180) was Roman Emperor from 161 to 180. He is known for his book, MEDITATIONS. He symbolized much of what was best about Roman civilization.

b

Joan Chandos Baez (1941) is an American folk singer and song writer. She is also a strong activist.

Sir James Matthew Barrie (1860 – 1937) was a Scottish author and playwright best known for his play, PETER PAN.

John Barrymore (1882 – 1942) was an American actor.

William Blake (1757 – 1827) was an English poet, painter, and printmaker from the Romantic Age. He lived in London his entire life.

Ralph Blum is a writer and cultural anthropologist who is the author of the successful Runes series, including THE BOOK OF RUNES, THE HEALING RUNES, and THE SERENITY RUNES.

Robert Brault is a freelance writer and writer of motivational quotes.

The Reverend Dr Thomas Bray (1658 – 1730) was an English minister who spent time in Maryland as an Anglican representative.

Sarah Ban Breathnach is the author of SIMPLE ABUNDANCE.

Felice Leonardo "Leo" Buscaglia (1924 – 1998) was an author, professor and motivational speaker. He was also known as "Dr Love" after the class he taught at USC. He spoke on PBS and had many best sellers.

Buddha (5th Century B.C.) was also known as Siddharta Guatama, born in what is now Nepal. He was a prince who renounced he life to experience suffering. He became enlightened and taught his followers about life called Buddhism. Buddha also is a title given to those who are enlightened.

c
Julia Cameron is the author of THE ARTIST'S WAY and several follow-up books. She is also a poet, playwright and filmmaker.

Joseph John Campbell (1904 – 1987) was an American author, mythologist and lecturer. He covered the human experience and comparative religions. He was the first to say: "Follow your bliss."

Albert Camus (1913 – 1960) was a French Algerian author, philosopher and journalist, who was awarded the Nobel Prize for Literature in 1957. His most famous book is the novel L'ÉTRANGER (The Stranger).

Dale Carnegie (1888 – 1955) was an American writer and lecturer and the developer of famous courses in self-improvement. His most famous book is HOW TO WIN FRIENDS AND INFLUENCE PEOPLE.

Carlos Casteneda (1925 – 1998) was a Peruvian-born American anthropologist and author. He wrote THE TEACHINGS OF DON JUAN.

Sir Winston Leonard Spencer-Churchill, (1874 – 1965) was a British politician and statesman known for his leadership of the United Kingdom during the WWII.

Julia Child (1912 – 2004) was an American chef, author, and television personality.

Doc Childre is a stress expert. He is the founder of the HeartMath System, considered by many to be the best in stress management.

Paul Coelho (1947) is a Brazilian lyricist and novelist.

Confucius (552 BCE) was a Chinese philosopher. K'ung Fu-tzu is the correct spelling of his name. Confucianism is the religion name for Confucius.

d
Dalai Lama is a Buddhist leader of religious officials of Tibetan Buddhism. The 14th Dalai Lama (July 6, 1935), was only formally recognized as the 14th on 17 November 1950, at the age of 15.

Charles Robert Darwin (1809 – 1882) was an English naturalist. He established that al species of life have descended over time from common ancestors. This theory is called evolution.

Leonardo DaVinci (1452 – 1519) was an Italian polymath: painter, sculptor, architect, musician, scientist, mathematician, engineer, inventor, anatomist, geologist, cartographer, botanist and writer.

Doris Day (1922) is an American actress and singer, and has been an outspoken animal rights activist since her retirement from show business.

Renee Descartes (1596 – 1650) French philosopher, mathematician, physicist and writer.

Desiderata "desired things" is a prose poem by German-American writer Max Ehrmann.

Rosaleen Diana Leslie Dickson, (1921) is an author, editor and journalist from Canada.

Charles Dickens (1812 – 1870) was the most popular British novelist of the Victorian era writing novels that gave voice to social reform.

Joan Didion (1934) is an American author best known as a novelist and essayist.

Walt Disney (1901 – 1966) was an American film producer, director, screenwriter, voice actor, animator, entrepreneur, entertainer, international icon, and philanthropist.

Benjamin Disraeli (1804 – 1881) was a British Prime Minister.

John Donne (1572 – 1631) was an English poet and minister best known for his love poetry and sonnets.

Dostoevsky (1821 – 1881) was a Russian writer and essayist, best known for his novels CRIME AND PUNISHMENT and THE BROTHERS KARAMAZOV.

Albus Dumbledore is the fictional headmaster of Hogwarts in the Harry Potter book series.

Wayne Dyer (1940) is an American self-help advocate, author, and lecturer.

e
Baroness Marie von Ebner-Eschenbach (1830 – 1916) was an Austrian writer. She is one of the most important German language writers in the 19th century.

Thomas Edison (1847 – 1931) was an American inventor, scientist, and businessman who developed many devices that greatly influenced life around the world, including the phonograph, the motion picture camera, and a long-lasting, practical electric light bulb.

Albert Einstein (1879 – 1955) was a theoretical physicist, philosopher and author who is widely regarded as one of the most influential and best known scientists and intellectuals of all time.

George Eliot/Maryanne Evans (1819 – 1880) was an English novelist and one of the leading writers of the Victorian era.

Ralph Waldo Emerson (1803 – 1882) was an American philosopher. He published many essays and spoke at many lectures. He is best remembered as a poet, lecturer and essayist. Also a leading member of the Transcendentalist movement.

Mary Englebreit (1952) is a graphic artist and children's book illustrator who launched her own magazine, Mary Engelbreit's Home Companion in 1996. She began her career by designing and creating greeting cards.

Epictetus (AD 55 – AD 135) was a Greek philosopher, born a slave in what is now modern day Turkey. He lived in Rome and then Greece. A student of his published all his writings in a book called DISCOURSES. He believed that all external events were controlled by fate.

Richard L. Evan (1906 - 1971) writer, producer, announcer and an apostle in the Mormon Church.

Antoine de St. Exupery (1900 – 1944) French writer and aviator. His most well known book is THE LITTLE PRINCE.

f
Anne Frank (1929 – 1945) is one of the most renowned and most discussed Jewish victims of the Holocaust. Her diary kept during WWII has become one of the world's most widely read books.

Benjamin Franklin (1706 – 1790) was one of the Founding Fathers of the United States. Franklin was a leading author and printer, politician, postmaster, scientist, inventor, civic activist, statesman, and diplomat.

Robert Frost (1874 – 1963) was an American poet.

g
Galileo (1564 – 1642) was an Italian physicist, mathematician, astronomer and philosopher.

Mohandas Karamchand Gandhi (1869 –1948) was the pre-eminent political and spiritual leader of India during the Indian Independence movement. He pioneered change through non violence.

Johann Wolfgang Goethe (1749 − 1832) was a German writer. His most well known work is FAUST.

Khalil Gibran (1883 − 1931) was a Lebanese American artist, poet and writer. He is best known for his 1923 book, THE PROPHET. Gibran is considered to be the third most widely read poet just behind Shakespeare and Lao-Tzu.

Ellen Goodman (1941) is an American journalist and award winning columnist.

Stephen Grellet (1773 − 1855) was a prominent French Quaker immigrant and missionary. He was born Etienne de Grellet du Mabillier. He met with many important dignitaries of the time.

Terri Grillemets (1973) creator of www.quotegarden.com largest online collection of quotes.

Elizabeth Gouge (1900 − 1984) was an English author of novels, short stories and children's books. One of her most well known novels is THE LITTLE WHITE HORSE.

h

Nathaniel Hawthorne (1804 − 1864) was an American novelist and short story writer.

Heraclitus (535 − 475 BC) was an ancient Greek philosopher from Ionia, on the coast of Asia Minor. Heraclitus is famous for his theory of change being central to the universe.

Donald Ross Henry (1933 − 2003) Father, husband, fireman and my father-in-law.

John Holland Henry (1960) Designer and my husband.

Elbert Hubbard (1856 – 1915) was an American writer, publisher, artist, and philosopher. He was an influential exponent of the Arts and Crafts movement and is, perhaps, most famous for his essay A Message to Garcia.

Harold Stacey Hulbert (1887) He was a doctor and expert witness who helped in several famous cases in the '20s and '30s.

i

j
David Star Jordan (1851 – 1931) was a leading eugenicist, ichthyologist, educator and peace activist. He was president of Indiana University and Stanford University.

Carl Gustave Jung (1875 – 1961) was a Swiss psychiatrist, an influential thinker and the founder of analytical psychology. Jung is often considered the first modern psychologist.

k
Omar Khayyam (1048 - 1131) was a Persian mathematician, philosopher, astronomer, physician, and poet.

Helen Adams Keller (1880 – 1968) was an American author, activist and lecturer. She was deaf and blind.

John Fitzgerald "Jack" Kennedy (1917 – 1963) was the 35th President of the United States. He served from 1961 until he was assassinated in 1963.

Martin Luther King (1929 – 1968) was an American clergyman, activist, and prominent leader in the African American civil rights movement. He is best known for being an iconic figure in the advancement of civil rights in the United States and around the world,

Elisabeth Kübler-Ross, M.D. (1926 – 2004) was a Swiss-born psychiatrist who studied near death experiences. Her famous book is ON DEATH AND DYING.

Jack Kornfield (1945) Buddhist teacher and author.

Harold S. Kushner is a prominent American rabbi.

l
Lao-tzu (6th century BC) means "old master". Many claim he may be a mythical figure, some that he really did live or was maybe multiple historical figures. He taught and wrote about the Tao.

John Lennon (1940 – 1980) was an English singer-songwriter who rose to worldwide fame as one of the founding members of The Beatles and, with Paul McCartney, formed one of the most successful songwriting partnerships of the 20th century.

Anne Morrow Lindbergh (1906 – 2001) was a pioneering American author and the spouse of aviator Charles Lindbergh. She wrote 13 books, among them, GIFTS FROM THE SEA.

Henry Wadsworth Longfellow (1807 – 1882) was an American poet and educator whose works include "Paul Revere's Ride" and "The Song of Hiawatha".

Father Larry Lorenzoni

James Russell Lowell (1819 –1891) was a poet, critic and diplomat.

Martin Luther (1483 – 1546) was a German and teacher who began the Protestant revolution.

m

Edwin Markham (1852 - 1940) was an American poet.

Margaret Meade (1901 – 1978) was an cultural anthropologist.

Mother Teresa (1910 – 1997), born Agnes Gonxha Bojaxhiu was a Catholic nun from Albania. For over 45 years she worked with the poor in India and in other parts of the world.

Edna St. Vincent Millay (1892 – 1950) was an American poet. She won the first Pulitzer Prize for poetry.

Seymour Miller/Jill Jackson - 20th century writer musician collaborators

Bob Moawad author of WHATEVER IT TAKES.

Claude Monet (1840 – 1926), was a founder of French impressionist painting, and the most consistent and prolific practitioner of the movement's philosophy of expressing one's perceptions before nature.

William Morris (1834 – 1896) was an English textile designer, artist, writer, and socialist associated with the Pre-Raphaelite Brotherhood and the English Arts and Crafts Movement.

n

Ralph Nader (1934) is an American attorney, author, lecturer and political activist.

Friedrich Wilhelm Nietzsche (1844 – 1900) was a 19th-century German philosopher.

Nell Newman (1959) is a former child actress who performed under the name of Nell Potts. She founded an organic food and condiment production company, Newman's Own Organics.

Isaac Newton (1642-1727), mathematician and physicist, one of the foremost scientific intellects of all time.

Jewahariah Nehru (1889 – 1964) was an Indian statesman who was the first (and to date the longest-serving) prime minister of India, from 1947 until 1964.

Willie Nelson (1933) American Country singer.

Reinhold Niebor (1892 – 1971) was an American theologian and commentator on public affairs. Niebuhr was the archetypal American intellectual of the Cold War era.

Christiane Northrup author of WOMAN'S BODIES, WOMAN'S WISDOM.

o
Conan O'Brien (1963) is an American television celebrity, comedian, and producer.

Osho (1931 – 1990) an Indian mystic and spiritual leader.

Ovid (43 BC – AD 17/18) was a Roman poet.

p
Pablo Diego José Francisco de Paula Juan Nepomuceno María de los Remedios Cipriano de la Santísima Trinidad Ruiz y Picasso known as Pablo Ruiz Picasso (1881 – 1973) was a Spanish painter and sculptor. He is best known for the Cubist movement.

Edith Mary Pargeter/Ellis Peters (1913 – 1995) was a British author of historical fiction. She also translated Czech books into English.

Blaise Pascal (1623 - 1662, Paris) was a French mathematician, physicist, inventor, writer and Catholic philosopher.

Sean Justin Penn (1960) is an American film actor and director.

Edith Piaff (1915 – 1963) was a French singer and cultural icon who became universally regarded as France's greatest popular singer.

Plato (428/427 BC – 348/347 BC)was a Classical Greek philosopher, mathematician, writer of philosophical dialogues, and founder of the Academy in Athens, the first institution of higher learning in the Western world. His mentor was Socrates and his student, Aristotle.

Price Pritchett (1941) Merger specialist.

Valentin Louis Georges Eugène Marcel Proust (1871 – 1922) was a French writer. He is best know for REMEMBRANCE OF THINGS PAST.

q
Anna Marie Quindlen (1953) is an American author, journalist and opinion columnist. Several of her novels have been made into movies.

r
Agnes Repplier (1855 – 1950) was an American essayist born in Philadelphia, Pennsylvania.

Chögyam Trungpa Rinpoche (1939-1987) also known as Trungpa Rinpoche, was the 11th descendent of important teachers in Tibetan Buddhism. Throughout his life, Trungpa Rinpoche sought to bring the teachings he had received to the largest possible audience.

Fred McFeely Rogers (1928 − 2003) was an American educator, minister and television host of MISTER ROGER'S NEIGHBORHOOD from 1968 to 2001.

Eleanor Roosevelt (1884 − 1962) was the First Lady of the United States from 1933 to 1945. She was married to Franklin Delano Roosevelt.

Theodore Roosevelt (1858 − 1919) was the 26th President of the United States. He is noted for his energetic personality, range of interests and achievements.

J.K. Rowling (1965) is the British author best known for the HARRY POTTER series.

Rumi (1207 − 1273), was a 13th-century Persian poet.

s

Jonas Edward Salk (1914 − 1995) was an American medical researcher best know for his development of the polio vaccine.

Albert Schweitzer (1875 − 1965) was a Franco-German (Alsatian) theologian, organist, philosopher, and physician.

Angela Schwindt is a home-schooling Mom in Oregon who coaches a performing unicycle team, the One Wheel Wonders.

Bernie Seigal, a doctor who is the author of several books on the relationship between the patient and the healing process as it manifests throughout one's life.

Seneca (3 BC – 65 AD) was a Roman Stoic philosopher, statesman, dramatist, and humorist. He was tutor and later advisor to emperor Nero.

William Shakespeare (1564 - 1616) was an English poet and playwright.

Shantideva (8th-century) was an Indian Buddhist scholar and author.

Lillian Smith 1897 – 1966) was a writer and social critic of the Southern United States, known best for her best-selling novel STRANGE FRUIT.

Marsha Sinetar is an organizational psychologist, mediator, and writer who for the past several years has been increasingly immersed in the study of self-actualizing adults.

Benjamin McLane Spock (1903 – 1998) was an American pediatrician. His book BABY AND CHILD CARE, was published in 1946 and became one of the best sellers of all time.

Tom Stoppard (1937) is an influential British playwright, knighted in 1997.

Jim Stovall is an American writer known for his novel, THE ULTIMATE GIFT. He is also blind and is an advocate for people with blindness.

Publilius Syrus (1st Century BC) was a Latin writer. He was a Syrian who was brought as a slave to Rome, but by his wit and talent he won the favor of his master, who freed and educated him.

t

Alfred Lord Tennyson (1809 – 1892) was Poet Laureate of the United Kingdom during much of Queen Victoria's reign and remains one of the most popular poets in the English language.

Thích Nhất Hạnh (1926) is a Buddhist monk, teacher, author, poet and peace activist now based in France.

Henry David Thoreau (1817 – 1862) was an author, poet and philosopher, plus a leading political activist. He is best known for the book, WALDEN.

Lily Tomlin 1939) is an American actress, comedian, writer and producer.

Harry S. Truman (1884 – 1972) was the 33rd president of the United States from 1945 to 1953.

Mark Twain (1835 – 1910) also known as Samuel Langhorne Clemens, was an American author and humorist. He is most known for his novels the ADVENTURES OF HUCKLEBERRY FINN and THE ADVENTURES OF TOM SAWYER.

u

v

w

William Arthur Ward (1921- 1994) author of Fountains of Faith, is one of America's most quoted writers of inspirational maxims.

John Wesley (1703 – 1791) was an Anglican cleric who is credited (along with his brother) for starting the Methodist Church.

Elie Wiesel (1928) is a Romanian-born Jewish-American writer, professor, political activist, Nobel Laureate, and Holocaust survivor.

Oscar Fingal O'Flahertie Wills Wilde (1854 – 1900) was an Irish writer, poet and playwright. He is best known for THE IMPORTANCE OF BEING ERNEST and THE PICTURE OF DORIAN GRAY.

William Wordsworth (1770 – 1850) was a major English Romantic poet who, with Samuel Taylor Coleridge, helped to launch the Romantic Age in English literature

Frank Lloyd Wright (1867 – 1959) was an American architect, interior designer, writer and educator.

y

z

the Zen Mama The Zen Mama Master, fictional character in HOW TO BE A ZEN MAMA.

Zhuangzi also known as Chuang Tzŭ (4th century BCE) was a Chinese Philosopher.

Jon Kabat-Zinn (1944) is a professor of mindfulness meditation as a technique to help people cope with stress, anxiety, pain and illness.

Do all the good you can,
in all the ways you can,
to all the souls you can,
in every place you can,
at all the times you can,
with all the zeal you can,
as long as ever you can.

~JOHN WESLEY

Acknowledgements

There are always many people to thank.

To my mother and father for their encouragement. Many, many thanks to my father for all his editing and constructive criticism. Many, many thanks to my mother for always being there with positive thoughts and advice.

To my new blogging friends: I would like to thank Jen, Sheila, Michelle, Angela, Julie, Lori, Michiko, Melissa, Jenny, Tess and Carol. I have great gratitude for your enthusiasm as you read my blog posts and for leaving such encouraging comments.

Thanks to Aunt Lowlie for the first quote book you gave me! It has always inspired me! Aunt Debbie, I remember when you started your feather business and that has inspired me to go after my dreams. To Aunt Suzie, thank you for the lovely times we spent in London together.

To my three boys, Max, Charlie and Oliver, for their encouragement. You are my inspiration for my writing. I love you!!

友谊

"Friendship"

If I can stop one heart from breaking,
I shall not live in vain; If I can ease
one life the aching, Or cool one pain,
Or help one fainting robin
Unto his nest again,
I shall not live in vain.

~EMILY DICKINSON

About the Author

Betsy Henry is a mom, wife and preschool teacher. She grew up in the suburbs of Chicago and went on to get her elementary education degree at Indiana University. She moved to Colorado in 1985 where her family had spent many happy family vacations.

When she's not drinking coffee, you can find Betsy reading, writing cooking, gardening and traveling with her family. She wrote her first book, HOW TO BE A ZEN MAMA, in hopes that other mothers will be able to stop worrying, let go and live happier lives. She lives with her husband and three boys in Littleton, Colorado.

Please read The Zen Mama's Blog at www.zen-mama.com.

> *Fill your paper with the*
> *breathings of your heart.*
> ~WILLIAM WORDSWORTH

MOTHER THERESA'S PRAYER

PEOPLE ARE OFTEN UNREASONABLE,
IRRATIONAL, AND SELF-CENTERED.
FORGIVE THEM ANYWAY.

IF YOU ARE KIND, PEOPLE MAY ACCUSE
YOU OF SELFISH, ULTERIOR MOTIVES.
BE KIND ANYWAY.

IF YOU ARE SUCCESSFUL, YOU WILL WIN SOME
UNFAITHFUL FRIENDS AND SOME GENUINE
ENEMIES. SUCCEED ANYWAY.

IF YOU ARE HONEST AND SINCERE
PEOPLE MAY DECEIVE YOU.
BE HONEST AND SINCERE ANYWAY.

WHAT YOU SPEND YEARS CREATING, OTHERS
COULD DESTROY OVERNIGHT. CREATE ANYWAY.

IF YOU FIND SERENITY AND HAPPINESS, SOME
MAY BE JEALOUS. BE HAPPY ANYWAY.

THE GOOD YOU DO TODAY, WILL OFTEN BE
FORGOTTEN. DO GOOD ANYWAY.

GIVE THE BEST YOU HAVE, AND IT WILL NEVER
BE ENOUGH. GIVE YOUR BEST ANYWAY.

IN THE FINAL ANALYSIS, IT IS BETWEEN YOU
AND GOD. IT WAS NEVER BETWEEN
YOU AND THEM ANYWAY.

Your Favorite Quotes:

The unexamined life is not worth living.
~PLATO

Your Favorite Quotes:

Be happy for this moment.
This moment is your life.

~OMAR KHAYYAM

Your Favorite Quotes:

Genius develops in quiet places, character out in the full current of human life.
~GOETHE

Your Favorite Quotes:

Life was meant to be lived, and curiosity must be kept alive. One must never, for whatever reason, turn his back on life.

~ELEANOR ROOSEVELT

Made in the USA
Charleston, SC
10 August 2015